Muscle Memory

M.E. Berkley

Muscle Memory

For Iris, for Paolo, for little girl lost
For the skeletons and souls in backyards
For take-backs, second chances, and hope
Always hope

Muscle Memory
ISBN 978 1 76109 279 4
Copyright © M.E. Berkley 2022

First published 2022 by
Ginninderra Press
PO Box 3461 Port Adelaide 5015
www.ginninderrapress.com.au

Contents

Part I: Iris

Moon child	11
To leave a pretty corpse	12
Westport	13
Folie à deux	14
I	15
II	16
III	17
Melancholia	18
Family crypt	19
Heir(ess)	20
Runaway	21
Violent bones, lying hands, forgiving tongue	22
Sunday	23
2076	24
Weave like the spider	25
Don't charge him with rape, charge him with murder	26
October	27
Friend, foe, woe	28
Lean in close	29
We weren't star-crossed, you never looked up	30
Cabin in the woods	31
Treasured home	32
Ascendant	33
Call your girlfriend	34
Sudden like lightning, slow like thunder	35
Capricorn sun, Taurus moon	36
Solis/Solace	37
Oh, to live amongst stars!	38
So mote it be	39
Iris	40

Part II: Atlas and the Sky Upon His Shoulders

Conscious slumber	45
Self-isolation/self-care	46
Delusion, transfusion, conclusion	47
Mend	49
Hysteric	50
Pleasure(able)	51
Wander-lost	52
Womb/tomb	53
Petrichor	54
Please stand behind the yellow line	55
Spill your guts, and other clichés	56
Two fruit, five veg, and a B12 vitamin	57
Atlas and the sky upon his shoulders	58
Planet A	59
Undone	61
Bloom	63
Penultimate promise	65
My blood, my water	66
Ever, ever	67
211	69
Manic pixie dream hurl	70
Lithi-yum	72
Exhale	73
A wish on an eyelash	74
Elastic Love	76
Right-eous	77
I, eye, why	78

Part III: Muscle Memory
  Tears for Paolo   81
  Kintsugi   83
  Lamentations   84
  Gestation/revelation   85
  Levonorgestrel   86
  Gospel/hostile   87
  14.04.21   88
  Ache   89
  Release   90

Part I

Iris

Moon child

No one knows me like the moon does.

The secrets I have shared with her
Under cold breath over bruised knees
Tell more of my soul
Than the months spent searching for home
In blades of grass and lungfuls of air.
Her light holds me like a lover
And I welcome that embrace
As the shore welcomes the sea.
I am pure again when I look upon her face
And she whispers healing songs,
Sent through the wind and the tide.

To leave a pretty corpse

If only
The nights I spent
With stomach growling
And teeth chattering
Could stop the bile
Rising
Each time I stare
Into a reflective surface

Sometimes
When the sun sets
I can't help
But be left
Feeling
At home in the dark
Because everyone is beautiful
With the lights off

Westport

I think about this beach a lot

My family spent Christmas in Connecticut
The winter after I tried to kill myself
We drove past the sandy shore
Where trees were skeletons
And a lone park bench
Sat like a lighthouse
Steady, strong

I think maybe in the afterlife I will be on this beach
I will walk its length until I know it
Like the moon knows the tides
And I will share with it
The secrets I first whispered
Out a car window when I was fourteen and depressed
I will sit on that bench
And feel the cool wind caress me
Not like a lover, but like a mother
One unlike the earthly one I was given
One who will tend to my soul
As a part of her own

Folie à deux

I know what it's like
To fill your pockets with rocks
And wade into the water

To take off your rings
Climb into your car
Turn the engine on
And close your eyes

Lock your children away
Stick your head in the oven
Breathe with final purpose

To make art is to suffer
To be a woman is woe
We bleed ink onto pages
Let the world suck us dry
Give all that we have
To be a part of something more
Because in our depths
We sense we are nothing
Without the madness that haunts us

The shadows that keep us up at night
Look like the sun to the others
And who are we
To take that light away

I

Little girl lost
Takes a bite from the apple
Trades her soul for the knowledge
Is cast out of the chapel

Water you weed you
It's only pulling teeth
And your lie is no better
Than the secrets you keep

Eyes beaten broken
See only what breaks
Turn kaleidoscope colour
With each pill that I take

Ashes to ashes
Dust to dust
Mind of mine
You stole my trust

II

A shot in the daylight
Will set off your fright
And you'll search for answers (unrequite)
But none bat an eye
When the sky is falling.

It catches you under water
Screams: act as I've taught you
Pull it together, you son or you daughter
It isn't today
That the sky is falling.

Perhaps I am losing my mind
I didn't think it would happen this time
But the more I dream the more I whine
Haven't you heard?
The sky is falling.

Lock away these secrets
It's only real if you speak it
You can't have peace but try to seek it
Behind your eyelids the sky
                keeps on
                          falling

III

I imagine her world is candy-coloured
And we are marshmallow men
She'll bite off our heads
And empty our pockets
To decorate her lilac sky
Everything shines here
She paints diamonds with her tongue
Across a field of jasmine.

And I'd leave her be
If I knew she could stay there
Chasing jelly butterflies
But the ice cream towers melt
And the gingerbread turns sour
I watch her teeth rot
And with her gummed mouth
Cry for a self long gone.

Melancholia

Shadows and shoestrings
Fill your gut bide your time
Shout or whisper 'the end is nigh!'
Curled toothpicks in your gums

And it shall come to pass
When the foot of your bed
And the blood in your mouth
Can't save you from the night

(I have such tired bones)

Family crypt

I want to be cremated.
I want to burn until I am pure again.
Let every last ash be a reminder
That I have no resting place.

Don't return me to mother earth,
She never loved me anyway,
So who am I to give her flesh
To feast upon and be nourished?

My bones belong as flames
As constellations belong to the sky,
So set me alight and watch
As I finally rest in peace.

Heir(ess)

They want me to fill my arms with a child
But my arms were only meant to hold
My own hair back
As I purge

Runaway

When I was a child
And the anger felt like suffocation
I would pack a bag and
maybe
Make it to the end of the street
Before turning back around

These days
When I pack my bags
I don't return so soon
But I still always seem
To find my way back

To the house with the green gates
And the knowing smirks
And the prayers hanging overhead
Like rainclouds
When you asked for sunshine

Violent bones, lying hands, forgiving tongue

If he lives in the sky
Then I'll bury myself deep
Beneath the heritage tree
That shadowed my childhood
From his scorching Sun

I'll farewell beloved constellations
And make home of cold earth
Where roots make delicate nooses
For my crooked sinner's neck

And when the rain falls
It will remind me
Of when he gave manna
To the Israelites
Only to let them toil
In a desert for   forty   more   years

If I get
Forty more years
My voice will not sing
A single praise above
But will call out
Songs of love and acceptance
To all the souls
Buried in their backyards

Sunday

Salvation found me
When I was young
He said 'come to me
And I will give you rest'
But all I got were
Shackles on the tongue
And a guilty ticking heart

2076

I learned to live behind closed doors
Where every house has a swimming pool
And every Sunday
Was spent down the street
On your knees
While Monday through Saturday
You chased with bloody footsteps
Through halls of padlocked smiles
The hope of a future far
From picket fences

Where every December
Candies stuck to braced teeth
And the pulling felt like when
The hairbrush met your skull
But your silence was rewarded
With a watch and a Nintendo

I count the property lines as I walk
To and from the train station
That I have walked to and from
For too many years
And from many things

One day
I will be on a beach
And for a moment
I will forget
Exactly how it felt
To love and be loved
By a gas
   light

Weave like the spider

There is a little part of my chest that was carved out many
    years ago.
Not my from my heart, but somewhere nearby, so that strong
    constant beat
Leaves an echo in the crater left by what was stolen from me.

Don't charge him with rape, charge him with murder

Birthdays have lost meaning for me,
I am still fifteen.
Still lying with my legs apart
Wet from his saliva
Afraid to move a muscle
Naked as the day I was born
Not knowing this was the day I died.

I didn't get a funeral.
I got birthday cards, cake, presents
Don't they know I'm just a ghost?
This shell you call daughter, sister, friend
Died on a teenage boy's mattress
Alone and afraid, and after saying 'no'.

October

When I was small
I liked to breathe hot air
Onto frosted glass
And draw
In the mist

Now I am grown
And I wonder
If the scars he carved into my skin
Were his pane of glass
And I his masterpiece

Friend, foe, woe

I expected it to be violent
A fist in a face
A knife to a throat
A scream in the dead of the night

But it crept up on me
Like the sun creeps over the horizon
And suddenly it is day

Suddenly I am smoke

Lean in close

God promised Abraham
As many sons as stars in the sky
And Abraham was in awe
For he believed the constellations countless.
But I have tallied the stars –
What else is there to do
When thrown on your back
And
violated
By the one you called
Lover.
Staring up is all you are left with
When your world turns upside down.

I sought solace in Orion's belt,
Pleaded for peace with the Big Dipper:
'Fiery spheres, ancient beings,
Share with me your wisdom!
The God of my childhood has forsaken me.
I know what is to burn,
I too am lightyears away.
Teach me to be whole once more,
Make me a promise
Not even God could keep.'

I await their celestial answer
Like the tides wait for the moon
To give them, at last, release.

We weren't star-crossed, you never looked up

He raises no hand,
That was never his way.
He was on his knees,
As if to pray.
Now sits up to speak,
Chair like throne,
'If you walk this path
You walk alone.'
As if that were
A thing to fear,
Have I not spent eternity
Alone, my dear?
My atoms roamed
The galaxy solo,
When made into woman
They remained hollow.
When paired with you
I found no solace,
Love's mighty bond
Just left me aweless.
If it frees me of him,
Then alone I'll be,
Not a single grievance
You'll hear from me.
I'd rather be deserted
Than smothered with lies,
When I hold my own hand,
His hold over me dies.

Cabin in the woods

One day
I will dive into a lake
Surrounded by mountains and a pine forest
And when I come up for air
I won't be breathing
You

Treasured home

Love does not live in the heart
But in the pit of one's stomach.
Deep amongst the bile and the waste,
Love grows and love churns.

Ascendant

Our love was wasted
Like fireworks
On a cloudy night

Call your girlfriend

I don't want to be
A name you scroll to on a screen
When she has fallen asleep
And your head feels full

I want to make your heart full

I want to hear your voice in the daylight
And be the first face you see
When you wake up
Every morning
For the rest of your
Life

I want to live in your soul
Not in a message box in
Your electronic attachment

I don't want to do this to myself

You don't want to do this
To her

Sudden like lightning, slow like thunder

Like the rose
We all wither and die

Capricorn sun, Taurus moon

I search for the stars that laid over me the moment of my birth.
I wonder what secrets they could tell if persuaded to share
That celestial knowledge they carry across the sky like
The wheels of a chariot carting treasure from Athens to Rome.

Solis/Solace

The moon has always been my mother
But I have had to learn to love the sun

Oh, to live amongst stars!

Bright shining secrets
Form paths overhead,
Listen as they glisten,
What whispers they share!
Stories of explosions
Each end but a beginning
Travelling an expanse,
They care for no compass,
Their sisters light the way.
Join hands to tell fortune
Of lives yet to be lived
Leave messages in planets
Of what has passed
And what will come to pass
It is it not all the same
To a celestial fire?
Death gives birth to life
In a universe unending
Where home is not a place
But an allegiance, a duty,
A promise to light the way
For souls searching the cosmos
To find purpose in another cycle
Of existence.

So mote it be

I lived so long in fear of
Below
I forgot that even the Seraphim
Had wings to shield their eyes
They were so in fear
Above

I took my scattered convictions
And ground them with mortar and pestle
Picked from my mind's growing garden
Basil, cinnamon, juniper
Stirred with charged moon water
And drank from a charmed cup

I found a truly unconditional love
In my own ability
To light a candle
When my mind was dark
Speak my own words
And manifest
A future limitless

Iris

I first saw her in purple
I don't remember seeing her again
I just remember it was fitting
That she wear such a colour
With a name like
                Iris

I was first confronted
With my own mortality
At five
When my grandfather's heart
Heaved for a final time
In a church, of all places

I cried for him
Then I cried for me
And prayed and prayed and prayed
For something beautiful over the horizon

I didn't cry like that again
Until I was nine
When a vessel in her brain
Ballooned and betrayed
Her life a decade short

I still think of her
At twenty-one
I think of the garden they planted
And her haircut
And how I quit
Every
single
thing
I ever started

And I still pray
Not to one god or another
But to the universe itself
That maybe there is
Something beautiful
Over the horizon
At least
Maybe there is
For Iris

Part II

Atlas and the Sky Upon His Shoulders

Conscious slumber

My grandmother once told me
That she woke with the sun.
I never could quite get myself
To leave my bed at dawn
I like too much
To lie in soft sheets
And hold onto fragments of dreams
That bring me a sense of belonging
I never find while awake.
That precious time
When I first open my eyes
And I still believe that what I dreamed
Was real
Existed
Happened
Those moments are what I live for.

Self-isolation/self-care

I have found a sort of patience
By cutting potatoes into eighths
And washing my hands every time
I walk through the door

I wake at the same time each day
I take my medications as directed
Stretch my hands to the sky
(I can't yet reach my toes)

I pick up books and don't put them down
Until I run out of pages to turn
I write as often as my mind will allow me
And to be honest, I'm being honest

Imagination bleeds into delusion
And I will tell my doctor (I will)
But I am finding moments of calm
And that is all I can ask for. For now.

Delusion, transfusion, conclusion

I have fallen in love
With faces and names
Voices and thoughts
And it thrills me

I live in a house by the beach
With sprawling acres
Of apple trees, lemon trees, orange trees
Or maybe clementines
And my four children
Run barefoot through fields
And roll down hills
And the sun shines
And the birds sing
And I am asleep when I am awake

I take cut pills
To shush the presence
Of a lover over my shoulder
But it never lasts
And they tell me to take bigger pills
Rounder pills
Chocolate gumdrop sharp pills

And I plan
And I plan
And I plan

I put a little dollar here
A bigger dollar there
And I will have my Kombi and my hammock
And the rosy cheeked children
And the lover holding my shoulder
Whom I wed in a forest
That never existed
Except when I lied
So they wouldn't pry the babe from my breast
Before I was ready
         up
     up
To grow up

I love him today
I love him tomorrow
One day he will know my name
And when the sound of it leaves his lips
I will smile in my mind

For that is where he lives.

Mend

These days
I eat my breakfast outside
And take my time with each bite
Let it sit in my mouth a while
Feel the sun on my face and the food on my tongue
Not thinking of any one thing or other

I am learning to
                     be

Hysteric

I wonder
If I stepped outside
And howled at the moon
Until the tears I could never cry
Rolled down and nourished the soil
Where I buried the skeleton of my firstborn
The one I never carried inside me
Would the neighbours listen?
Or would they roll down
Their curtains
Shut in
Shut in
Shut in
The mother wolf lives in the forest
A land far from here.

Pleasure(able)

I have opened my life
To earthly sins
By opening my legs

At first it hurt
And my voice was too quiet
But I am learning

And I want to keep learning
Until I can feel again
Without remembering
How gratification was turned
So sour
So young

Wander-lost

I have carried these tan lines
Across my back and shoulders
Since I returned from the desert
In September.
They've barely faded a shade
And I wonder
If I will be stripey forever.
The borders closed in April
And though I hated the weight
Of Nevada summer air
What I wouldn't give
To be on an adventure again.
I think perhaps
I have rose-coloured eyes
At the back of my head
For I know that every time
I am far away
I only long for home

Womb/tomb

I have no green thumb
But I have quite enjoyed
The succulent and the little terrarium
That sit beneath my window sill
Catching the sun as it rises each morn.
They are starting to brown
And I know I don't have long left with them
But beauty is always fleeting
At least that is what I tell myself.
Am I a bad mother
If I didn't want my children
Until they landed in my lap
Wrapped in newspaper blankets?
Perhaps the strongest love
Grows not from desire
But from circumstance
And the falling is more
Like climbing

Petrichor

I remember this cheesy quote
About learning to dance in the rain
And I could laugh and scoff
But there may be some wisdom
In celebrating the storm
After all
It always passes

Please stand behind the yellow line

I used to dream of a skyscraper
The city lights humming me to sleep
But now I long for the ocean
To be caressed by icy waves

I lost my soul on a train track
And would quite like to find it again
But the moss has grown over
And the tracks turned to rust

I just can't stand the suburbs
The in-between-ness of them
Too far from mother earth's embrace
Too close to the fence next door

I want too much, I know this
More than my hand can grasp
But I think this makes me human
And I am learning to embrace that

Spill your guts, and other clichés

My father says I share too much
To a cruel world
Waiting to swallow me whole
But I want my mind-book open
Even if they tear the pages
They are mine to gift
And if I let them sit
For decades more
Inside my heart-library
They will start to smell
And gather dust

And I hate cleaning

Two fruit, five veg, and a B12 vitamin

I never liked my leafy greens
But I have grown to love
The taste of sustenance
That comes from the soil

The sharp   crack
Of a stick of carrot
Snapped between my teeth
Offers more than the
Melt-in-your-mouth
Cow pus
I used to rely on
For nutrition

Mother Earth has always
Given exactly what I need
I simply had to learn
To pick the fruit
They told me was forbidden
When it was really
Grown with love

Atlas and the sky upon his shoulders

Why
Do they always depict him
Holding the earth?
He held up the sky
For Gods' sake.
Is such a burden not enough?
To be shouldered the weight
Of the fate of all that live
By keeping their beloved
Clouds and constellations
From tumbling down
On ungrateful faces?

When they remember me
(If they remember me)
I hope they at least
Remember right

Planet A

I dream all day
Of where the forest meets the sea
And a town where they choose
Muslin over plastic
Roots over fruit
Sunlight over candlelight

Does it even exist
When my eyes are open?
A world where my footprints
Are washed away with the tide
Not fossilised in cement
For my great-great-grandchildren
To come across with magnifying glasses
And label malum homo sapien

Will they learn to breathe
In cities under water?
Finding that Atlantis
Was just the big apple
Before we took too great a bite
(The skin caught in our teeth
Yet we couldn't determine its source)

When did we become deaf
To our mother's cries?
We didn't –
We cut out our eardrums
And sold them for a piece
Of chewing gum
And a lotto ticket
So we would be too busy
To do a damn thing
About the oil in pelican beaks
Or the carcinogens in baby powder

 I sit still as a tree trunk
And wait for them to bring their chainsaws
Which I will swallow whole
And thank them for their gift
With a shiny
           gold
                  coin

Undone

For so long I imagined
Life's journey lived
On my own

A tiny house
On a patch of grass
By the ocean

My own company
Jars of lentils
A sprinkle of salt

But I metamorphed
I grew wings
And longed for a fellow moth

To seek out light
In a world gone dark
And buzz in its warmth

Hold my hand
Fly beside me
My heart is too full

To carry the weight
Of bountiful joy
Forever solitary

I want to give you
Everything   and
Then   some

When
      will
we
    meet
?

Bloom

I was born on a Wednesday
And this destined me to a life of woe

But I was born again
In a place where there are no days

Not from sermons or holy water
From my blood cells and split ends

My own two hands
Digging through the dirt

Of the grave where they buried me
So they could write on my headstone

'Child of woe, she cannot grow
She forsook her Holy Father

Damned now forever
She'll never know, this child of woe

The great love of heaven
The fear of omniscience

She has no seat at our table
Till she learns to spit repentance'

Their shadows follow me
Wishing to be the one to make me turn

But I am no table
I am life itself

I took my woe
And gave it a home

Far from my shores
Where it will leave me alone

And I dance in the forest
Weightless

I shine so bright
There is no room for shadows

The dirt beneath my fingernails
Is a reminder

That flowers
Must break
Through soil
In order
to
bloom

Penultimate promise

I am a cherry blossom tree
In the shade of a great mountain
I am a quiet stream
Running through an untouched forest
I am the salty wind
Blowing seas from the east
I am a silent whisper
Secrets yet to be told
I am the Divine Feminine
Shakti rising up my spine
I am the golden life force
Inside every living thing
I am those I hate
I live in them, and they in me
I am one
You are one
We are one
It is won

My blood, my water

There is love in ancient wisdom
Truths passed down mother to daughter
The combining of two herbs
To cure an ache in-between temples
We lost our way along the way
But I believe we will circle back
To the women's circles beneath
Laurel trees and constellations
Fire light offering guidance
When did we forget
That our bones
Are made of chalk
And our souls
Live between our eyes?
I hold you in my arms
As if you were my own
You are my own
And I am yours.

Ever, ever

Nostalgia sticks, heavy, to the roof of my mouth
When I listen to the sound of space

I used to fold myself into a paper crane
And be still as a stare
Waiting for someone to pull me apart
Smooth out the wrinkles on a marble countertop
Place me gently in a frame on a wall
With a little plaque, reading:
Prolonged exposure to the sun
Could never turn me blind

And wanted to move to Canada
Be far away from anyone who knew my name
I'd make up a new one and wear it
Like a child wears cardboard on their birthday
Then throws it away when the fear of getting old
Chips their teeth

I wanted I wanted I wanted
To live in a cabin the forest
With me, myself, and I
My soul still lives there but my heart
My ugly, beaten heart
Wants more
A half to my whole
A sweet clementine kiss
A thriving name I'd wear like a tattoo

And I'll always scream the words of Booster Seat
Even when years of indiscretions catch up
To names I will never meet but once loved

I find my home in the words of others
And hold out hope
That someone will find their home
In mine

211

I could spend all my money
On guitars I can't play
To impress some guy who
Doesn't even know my name
Will it fill the lover-shaped hole
I carved out of my own chest
With a pair of garden shears
Still dirty from the pruning
Of my body's garden?
Too big to be loved just yet
I spent hours each day
Finely trimming away at it
To make room for validation

Manic pixie dream hurl

Maybe one day
I will be sitting in a café
And I will catch your eye from across the room
You will walk over and ask
About the ashtray on my arm
And I won't pull away when you touch it
Unsolicited

We will take walks along the river
Where you tell me, in depth,
About your theories you've plagiarised
From Freud or Nietzsche or
The back of a cereal box
You don't ask about mine
But you assume I have a personality
I have tattoos and coloured hair
So there must be some tragic past
That makes me interesting
But not more interesting than you

I make all the right faces
In the bedroom
The living room
On the kitchen counter
And you feel satisfied that
I am filling some sort of hole in your life
(A role that may be better suited to a psychotherapist
But I don't open my mouth long enough
To make such a suggestion – your eyes get that
Glazed look
When you hear my voice so best leave it)

At some point I float off into the clouds
It is a deep tragedy you heal with a
Younger, slimmer model
Who uses the rest of my pink shampoo
When you fuck her in the shower
And loan her my nose ring
So if she squints just right
There's no need to take down
The photos you took for our three day anniversary

Lithi-yum

I am sick in the stomach
From riding this cycle
They love me at the top
When I throw my wallet at the bartender
And bounce around like a gumball
The leave me at the bottom
When sheets are my second skin
And pills are doled out in rations
The fleeting moments in-between
Are mostly just confusion
A longing for the
(But destructive)
Elevation which brings me friends in handfuls
And praise while chewing glass
They adore the tight-rope walk
Keen eyes watch my balancing act
I hold my breath for weeks a time
To be the right shade of violet
But my lungs are corrupted
I must let them heave
And the air that carries me back down
To concrete and bloodstains
Leaves an ever sour taste
On the tongues of those
Who have never had to pick up the pieces

Exhale

Where do I go?
Back to the arms of the one who doesn't love me
There is a comfort in his stubble and sweat
That I gladly trade
For hope of a better affliction
As my fears trickle down my spine
That no one will ever hold me
Choosing not to let go
When the novelty has worn off
And the moon hides behind a cloud

Why did I keep expecting you to show up on my doorstep?
Now my lips taste like cinnamon and my lungs cry out –
'Who is the real victor here?'

Lovers cannot all be roses
And lovers cannot all be thorns

A wish on an eyelash

The first boy I ever cried over
Taught me pain through indigo lies

But you made my eyes swell
In a thousand more hellish ways

I ran 3,000 ugly kilometres
Away from your indecision

But I can't get you off my heart
Or tell you what's on my mind

I count regrets from that morning
You kissed my cheek before you left

I would have held you closer
Had I known what was coming next

If you had stayed I would have stayed
And I wouldn't know the love

Of a sun setting over the ocean
And a pit where I should have hope

I trace your name in salt water
The kind that kisses my cheeks

The way you once did
On a morning when I still believed

We could grow a garden together
And taste fruit, fresh, before

It all rots
        in
            the
                end

Elastic Love

Why do I revert
To my reckless ways
Each time I think of how
You told me I'd be on your mind
All day
After the first night I spent
Next to you in your too-small bed

When I spilled my heart too soon
You mopped up the mess so
Casually
Tossed me aside like a paper doll
Still crinkled from the last
Young boy who didn't want
To care for a spiky, heavy,
Good-for-nothing soul like mine

Right-eous

I'd like to send a big ol'
FUCK YOU
To the boy who made me feel things
When I thought I'd never feel again
I hate that you're a good person
But would a good person do what you did?
How do I hold you in such
High regard
When you folded me like a napkin in your lap
And wiped your lips clean
Of a meal you ordered
But didn't want to pay for

I, eye, why

I shouldn't have told you the things that I told you
Unravelled my soul like it was bubblegum
For you to spit out when the flavour ran sour
I should have played the part
Held you and blown you and
And
And
I shouldn't have scared you off
By being fucking human
Raw and unreliable
Like a meteorite crashing the surface
Of your picture of what we could be
I'm sorry
The apology is not for you
It's for me
Tasting vulnerability
And taking a tactical spew
In the gutter that is
What could have been

Part III

Muscle Memory

Tears for Paolo

The holidays have your name wrapped up in beer wrappers
    and cigarette butts
I smoked my last one tonight and I thought of you
My lungs will heal and my heart will beat stronger
It will beat for yours that could not face another year
It will remember the train ride home when
We swapped antidepressants and sat in comfortable silence
The time you made a seat next to you in that hall where
I knew no other face and you made it a home
You made every hall a home
You found me a ride back to the city and laughed about my
    jokes about the stars
You made every star a home
And now it will be your forever place
When the nicotine cravings come ringing at my door I will
    not let them in
But make them a bed in a place far from here
Tuck them in goodnight
An eternal slumber like yours
I wish you were awake
But you deserve rest
A home where you can shine
I see your face in every sunset and moonrise
I catch the train alone these days
I take the right antidepressants
When I remember to, at least
And this time of year will always carry
Little remnants of a falling from grace
And a rising from closed doors

My tears for you took six months to mature
And the salt in the wound is sweet
It tells me to look at every sunset and moonrise
With the eyes of a sinner
Who knows not the love of a father
But that of a friend
A true friend

Kintsugi

I wanted the little avocado seed
A pit inside my womb
A growing force within my very being

I am not yet ready to see your face
Try as I might I cannot be what you need
Forgive me for my shattered pieces
And I will place them back together with gold
An ancient art
I will make this body a home
And protect you from this world

I wanted you little seed
But you did not want me

Lamentations

Do I drown my sorrows
Or are they drowning me
Cold hands against my throat
An ocean of carvings against my organs
I wanted to give you my bones

Gestation/revelation

Stability is an island far from here
I swim against currents to catch a glimpse
Of coconut trees and crystal waters
But my head goes under and I swallow salt

There will never be a perfect time
To hold you in my arms
But now is not the right time
My skin is peeling and my mind plays solitaire
On a table with half the legs sawed off

I poison my lungs against my better judgement
I'm trying (so hard, so hard)
To give up my vices two by two
To make more room for you oh you

We will never be alone if we have each other
But I want more for you
So I will wait
With the patience of a sailor
Who knows the horizon
Like Cleopatra knew the snake
Purposeful bite
Meaningful spite
I carry you in each wave
And wait and wait and run late
For currency and past mistakes

I will take my time for you

Levonorgestrel

They said I might throw up
And I'd have felt better if I had
Purged my regret in a toilet bowl
They said I might bleed early
And I count down the days
Until I pee on a stick and see
If the universe grants me a take back
I'll have a chance every waning moon
But it doesn't make losing you less heavy
You stick to the roof of my mouth
Like the dried sandpaper of breathless nights
This is the second time
The first was a delusion
Not made any less real
By my missing cycle and tender breasts
I crave them now
They would have been actual this time
Factual
In fact
Emma had her baby
A girl whose birthday is three days before mine
I wonder if Carla had hers
Or if she was brought grief in stacking shelves
Empty again
I want so badly
I crave
I desire
I cannot determine if it is selfish
Or something bigger than myself
I am so empty
Again

Gospel/hostile

I think I know
Why Jesus wept
At the loss of Lazarus
When he knew
He was hours away
From being reunited

He did not weep the loss
Of a friendship
But reflected
On his own mortality
He knew what was to come
For himself

I wish I'd had the foresight
I wouldn't have held on so tightly
To a glass worth breaking
In order to feel
                  alive again

14.04.21

What I would give
To go back

Kissing in the kitchenette
Meeting up for last cigarette
Exchanging higher powers
Talking on the phone for hours
Came to see you everyday
Hide and seek games were played
Overstaying more than welcome
Over-wearing the same old denim

But time is linear
And I can't forget

Hour-long showers
Never bought me flowers
Sleep schedule a mess
Only touched to get undressed
Fall asleep and wake alone
Never answer your fucking phone
The company of a bong hit
A high became your mistress

I long for you
But I don't need you

Ache

My heart is too full
It makes my mind blind
Overlook
Overlook
Overlook
Forgive another indiscretion
Tempt fate a little more
Perhaps we were
                star-crossed
(It's bullshit)
Sing along to all the songs
I never could relate
Until now
I always did want
What I can't have
And force a future
So hard it
        shatters
And bloodied hands
Rebuild alone
A space to call home

Is it a home without your wordless love?

Release

I trace the space
Where you laid your head
Your scent is gone now
I reclaim my bed